Syntax & Personality

syntax reveals personality.
change of syntax = shift in personality.

ANATOMY

OF

MELANCHOLY

AND OTHER POEMS

4/14

ALSO BY ROBERT WRIGLEY

ANATOMY

OF

MELANCHOLY

AND OTHER POEMS

ROBERT WRIGLEY

PENGUIN POETS

PENGUIN BOOKS
Published by the Penguin Group
Penguin Group (USA) Inc., 375 Hudson Street,
New York, New York 10014, USA

USA | Canada | UK | Ireland | Australia | New Zealand | India | South Africa | China
Penguin Books Ltd, Registered Offices: 80 Strand, London WC2R 0RL, England
For more information about the Penguin Group visit penguin.com

First published in Penguin Books 2013

LIBRARY OF CONGRESS CATALOGING-IN-PUBLICATION DATA
Wrigley, Robert, 1951–
[Poems. Selections]
Anatomy of melancholy and other poems / Robert Wrigley.
pages cm
Poems.
ISBN 978-0-14-312307-1
I. Title.
PS3573.R58A83 2013
811'.54—dc23
2012038722

Printed in the United States of America
1   3   5   7   9   10   8   6   4   2

Set in New Caledonia with Topaz
Designed by Ginger Legato

The author would like to express his gratitude to the
Bogliasco Foundation, for a residency in the spring of 2011,
at the Liguria Study Center, in Bogliasco, Italy,
where a number of these poems were written.

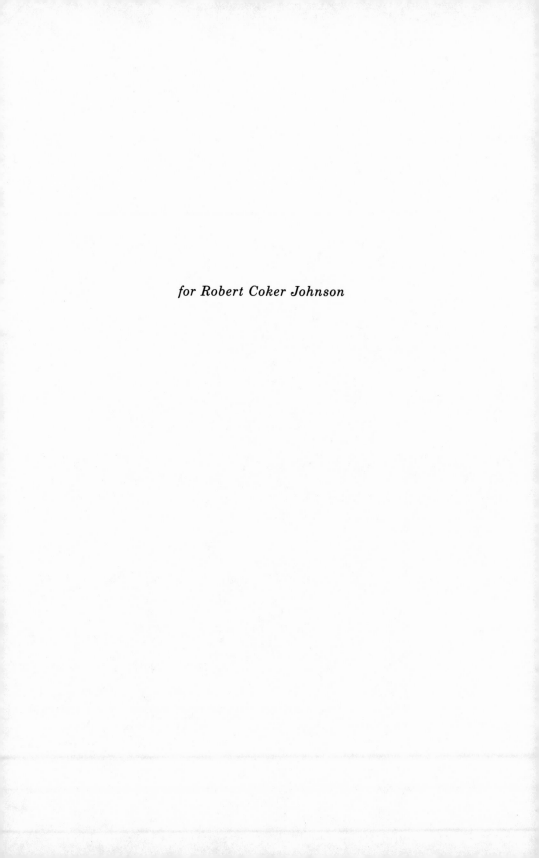

for Robert Coker Johnson

CONTENTS

PART THREE

DARK BLUE MOUTH

ANATOMY
OF
MELANCHOLY

AND OTHER POEMS

"This *Melancholy* of which we are to treat, is a habit, a serious ailment, a settled humour, as Aurelianus and others call it, not errant, but fixed: and as it was long increasing, so, now being (pleasant or painful) grown to a habit, it will hardly be removed."

—Burton

"Melancholy in this sense is the character of Mortality."

—Burton

"If any man except against the matter or manner of treating of this my subject, and will demand a reason of it, I can allege more than one; I write of melancholy, by being busy to avoid melancholy."

—Burton

"A nightingale dies for shame if another bird sings better."

—Burton

"So be it, then. It isn't all that bad."

—Szymborska

PART ONE

IN THE WHORL OF THE EAR OF ONE

TRIAGE

Scarred by a long-gone buck's rubbing,
shoved westward by his develveting grind,
the aspen had always leaned, and I had thought
many times I should stake it up, straighten it out,

but I never did. Then last week's several heavy
feet of snow became rain, and under that weight it split
at the buck's scar and bent to the ground,
and I was bereft. But in my regret I hauled

through the snow a hundred feet of ropes,
a come-along, a pair of steel pintle hooks,
and a five-gallon bucket of hopeful arborist's
paraphernalia. I tied it off to a stouter tree,

winched it upright again, braced it with a two-by-four
plank notched and swaddled at the notched end
in inner tube ribbons, then guyed it off to the fir
that was the engine of its reascension.

Afterward I plastered black tar around its wound,
wound a bandage of grafting tape over the tar,
and covered the tape in a green vinyl sleeve
against the winter yet to come. And every day,

in order to offer such apologies as I can,
I visit it. Sometimes, like the other day, I sit with it,
put an arm around it, and describe the motions
of its leaves in spring and summer,

and especially in its glorious fall:
how its gold shimmers, and how sometimes
a leaf will loose itself and fly the ten yards
to the porch of my shack and settle on a chair,

or in the cold October rains plaster itself
to a window like a kiss. That day I also explained
the next step in our treatment. How once
it is leafed out and green again, I will,

using the same rope that righted it, fasten
that rope at the height of my knee, at the strong
unbroken butt of it just below the buck's black scar,
and winch it a bit more upright yet, until,

by high summer, as straight as nearly any tree
around it, it will stand. Soon the seat of my pants
was wet from the snow and I was shivering,
but still I didn't want to go. I stood

and stroked the dressing around its wound
and resolved to come back from my shack
that afternoon, to read it a poem or two—
not my own, certainly not this one, but maybe

"The Wellfleet Whale" or "The Trees,"
in which "their greenness is a kind of grief"—
though I have not done so yet. "Begin afresh,"
I think this afternoon. "Last year is dead."

Larkin, I think, would have thought me a fool;
Kunitz, maybe not so much. Though I noticed,
in the divot where I'd sat beside it, a puddle
my own face regarded me from. I was empty-handed

and knew neither poem, the long nor the short,
by heart. Only the end of the Kunitz:
"Like us," it goes, "disgraced and mortal,"
from the puddle, said my face.

[handwritten margin note:] a conversation by poets who are no longer alive

The steer has found, among the mud
and diminishing islands of snow,
a cropped-off but less coagulate expanse
where it can lie and sleep awhile.

From where I watch, I can see
the quiver of an ear, a hind hoof
gently twitching, the ordinary mammalian
evidence that it is dreaming. But of what?

I wonder. Fields of tall grass forever?
A hay crib Jesus dispensing infinite fodder?
Or maybe not of food at all but the litheness
of its cousins, the deer and the elk,

those dreams that materialize each night,
when it must merely doze in the darkness,
vigilant, awaiting, once again, the light,
so that it might, as it does now, dream.

Though it may be in this way I diminish it.
It may be the cowbird, just a moment ago
having alighted on its broad neck, is Nyx,
consort of Erebus; that it dreams the day

is the night. Or perhaps the cowbird is no bird
at all, but the dream, and the dream is flying.
And what of me then? Even in its sleep
it may be aware of the presence of the maker

of fences, bringer of the gun, conjurer
of the high-backed truck and the hunchbacked
butcher, builder of the gut pile the ravens
and magpies will celebrate, for as long

as the furtive night dogs will allow, though now,
in sun and full sleep, it fears not, as it lifts
and pumps its enormous wings and soars
over the vast brown and white body of the earth.

CENOTAPH

Never especially inclined mathematically, my father,
days past his eightieth birthday, calculated the following:

if the names of all the dead, military and civilian alike,
of every nationality, from his war—the good one—

were blasted into granite, as were those of only
the American soldiers who had perished in the bad one, mine,

the resulting monument would be almost a mile long
and a hundred feet deep. Setting aside the engineering challenges,

he believed the greater problem was the names. Sixty million,
he ciphered, though I don't know how. His imagined monument,

a project no greater than the interstate highway system
or the dams across the nation's rivers, could take decades

to erect. No more than Rushmore or Crazy Horse.
And yet who would have envisioned such a task?

I remember how, the night of the first moon landing,
he stood in his backyard in the heart of the heart of the country,

straining through binoculars to see what could not be seen
but was. Now ten years past his monumental calculations,

the only numeral that matters to him is 2. We are not sure why.
Perhaps because my sister and I are two. As are he

and our mother, her failing eyes and gentle hands. And therefore
"two" is the answer to every problem the young neurologist poses,

a physician not much older than my own children,
none of whom ever lived through something called the draft.

My father does not know what year we are in or the name
of our current president. Even the names of his grandchildren

are lost to him sometimes, and if we were to ask
that name by which he calls himself, we fear that, too,

may be gone. He does not know, and probably never did,
the word *cenotaph*, though the memorial he once imagined

would have been just that, an empty tomb.
Father, let me estimate the dead for you:

it has been and will be everyone. Let us understand
that mountains are—like plains and swamps,

like rivers and oceans—death and life factories, forges from which
come numberless souls, residents on a spinning blue cenotaph

that without us has no name nor need of one.
These were the dead of a single war, these the dead

of the others. And here are those who died, as we say, in peace,
some whose lives have faded within them until they are

only the names and numbers they had been known by.
And here is where they were, beneath a cyclical moon,

which bears through the universe some footprints and a flag.

FRIENDLY FIRE

Is it even possible not to dream,
or not remember what one dreams of,
all the while a loop of endless music
going round and round in the mind? Last night,

every time I woke, it was "Moonlight Serenade,"
a song first recorded twelve years before
my birth—two weeks before my father's
seventeenth birthday—then rereleased four years

later, in 1943, the middle of his Navy stint,
as a "V-Disc." V for Victory, of course.
All night long, the melody's mild clarinets,
muted trumpets in jazzy counterpoint.

It did not come from nowhere, though,
this Glenn Miller classic, a four/four fox-trot.
I remember its red, white, and blue label,
from the Special Services Division, Music

Section of the War Department, a relic.
For an hour last night, my wife and I lay in bed
and spoke of our fathers. Hers, who'd said
if she'd been among the protestors at Kent State

she too would have deserved to be shot,
and mine, who in a singular act of anger
had broken a record I thought I loved.
In what way is one shaped by such a thing?

she wondered. Had anyone ever said to me
anything like what her father said to her?
And I told her no, although I thought of
Fresh Cream, the album mine had broken.

I'd been trying to learn the Clapton solo
on "I Feel Free," sitting with my guitar
before the speaker. I'd gone away, forgetting
the record there, and came back just in time to see it

shatter against a wall. They're both love songs.
In his, the man sings to his beloved in the light
of the moon; in mine, in the end, she is the sun.
Now my father's almost ninety. He wouldn't remember

having done such a thing, and I have no interest
in reminding him. We were at war in 1967.
He was just home from work. It is unclear
which of us was more miserable in his life then.

My mother promised she would buy me
a new one. My father reclined in his chair
to wait for dinner, before he dressed
and left for his second job, selling cars.

It is unclear if the money he made those nights
was necessary, though I think his absence was.
I did not think last night of his love for Glenn Miller.
I was not aware as my wife and I drifted into sleep

that "Moonlight Serenade" was loosed in my mind,
though I recalled this morning it was there
at each of my brief and sleepy awakenings.
And as it was all night, so it has been all day.

Clarinets and muted trumpets, managing
to be both melancholy and Caucasianally cool.
I remember he closed his eyes and seemed asleep
in his chair. I remember my mother's promise

and the single proviso she extracted from me:
that I say not a word of it over dinner.
And so I seethed and said nothing else either,
which must have made it, from her point of view,

among the most successful and pleasant
of our dinners in those days. She had left
Glenn Miller spinning, the changer arm up,
so that the song played again and again,

as it has in my mind for fifteen continuous hours now,
wordless through that day's stewed beef heart
and mashed potatoes, and through my lunch today as well—
some yogurt and fruit, a handful of nuts,

for now I am sixty, and while it is unclear
if I have any interest in reaching the age my father is,
I go on as though it were perfectly clear.
In 1967, he'd begun the long fall from faith,

believing never in God but somehow
in the nation, while I'd been spared any sense
of the holiness of either. Imagine an hour passed,
dinner eaten, my father having showered

and put on a tie, "Moonlight Serenade" still
and now eternally going. My mother tosses
a dish towel over her shoulder, and they dance
a few steps around the kitchen. I can see them

from the living room where I sulk and glare.
It must have been that day, in the midst
of rage and woundedness and fruitless stewing,
that his song became so deeply etched in my memory.

A moment ago I called it up from a computer file—
no vinyl, no tape, no disc at all, another victory
for technology, like virtual memory or unmanned drones—
and it unrolled from the speakers exactly

as I've been hearing it for a whole night and half a day,
its now primitive recorded nature preserved
almost perfectly, but for the absence of the needle's hiss.
In those days you either paid no attention to it

or else never dreamed it would go away.
If you are old enough to remember records—
forty-fives, seventy-eights, and thirty-three LPs—
you might also remember the ghost that lived

at the gleaming ungrooved lip of them, the way,
two or three seconds before the music began,
you heard its first notes coming. No such ghost
in the digital version, just the melody's clarinets,

the muted brass in counterpoint. What he said
and what he did: did either ghost itself into being first,
into place in his father's mind? Did he know
what he would say or do before he said or did it?

It came into the world and could not be undone
or unsaid, but was it unforgivable? Either from certainty
or misery, in the end it does not matter. From Old
Testament wrath or intolerable, petulant rage,

it does not go away. One cannot make it not be,
it was and it is. One can forget it with age
and infirmity or take it to the grave unresolved.
How fortunate for me, my father alive, and attached

to this memory in a sidelong way to music.
Last night's moon was waning and invisible
behind clouds, but still its light glowed
through the bedroom window. No one ever said

anything like that to me. No father ever loved
a daughter more than my wife's loved her.
The original title of "Moonlight Serenade"
was "Now I Lay Me Down to Weep," and the opening line was

"Weep for the moon, for the moon has no reason to glow now."
A flea-bitten symbol, a hackneyed metonymy for love,
that moon, a lyric trope retooled for a happier slant,
and thus made worthier in the end of victory, a word

no longer part of the vernacular of war. Eventually
the war ends, you bury your father. Eventually nothing
he said matters. Shame rots, scar tissue isn't visible
on the psyche's skin, you forget you tried to forgive,

you feel free to talk about it or you don't. Now
a song goes round and round for good reasons
or for none at all, and many songs are about love.
Glenn Miller vanished in December 1944, somewhere

over the English Channel. Some historians believe
his plane was hit by unused incendiaries jettisoned
from Royal Air Force bombers, his death,
in other words, caused by the actions of his own.

The current turns a shoaly lace of pebbles
in the shallows. They rattle *tick* and *tack*
and ring; they sing hosanna to the afterlife of sand.
Sun off a smolt in the kingfisher's beak
is a jewel its wings can live by. Its eye's black
and wary before it's gone. Runoff rubble
holds a rib cage against a rock. The land

contributes everything, leaves and beasts
and mountains bit by bit. A tiny bird's nest bobs
in an eddy, a blue egg-shard like a scrap of sky
on board. Polished cedar knuckle, a knob
of pine root, an amputated limb, a stob.
The sun in the west throws shadows east,
and a single vaporous cloud's going by.

From there it can see Montana
and beyond. An hour stacking river rock
one cannot be held accountable for. Applause
and kudos, clack the pebbles. The heron's stalk,
hunger's Zen, the river's long, liquid clock
and oceanward snowmelt extravaganza.
Then there's elsewhere: everyone else also in its claws.

A mail of mud
from his den's dried
along his back and side,
and he would,

if he raised his snout,
catch my scent,
except he's too intent,
tearing the rotten wood out

of an old pine stump,
to notice anything
but hunger's gnawing
and his own low grunts.

The long night
winter was makes me
feel for him no envy
whatsoever, and though I might

have wished not to be
so bothered by its snows
and cold, its blows
and drifts and difficulties,

none of these now seems . . .
well, unbearable, so to speak.
Whatever he is, he isn't weak,
as the stump's smithereens

make clear, but famished.
I hold the slingshot taut.
He's too close here and ought
to find another stump to ravish.

That's my thinking, at least,
though what right I possess
to this land still is less
than his need for a grubby feast.

So instead I yell *Hey*,
loud and bellowish as I can,
and he leaps half a man
high and runs away

a little ways, then stops,
turns to see, and rises
to his hind legs, surmises
I'm nothing much, adopts

a casual pose, and sits.
He licks a forepaw's pad,
so that the top of his head
is what the half-inch hex nut

slung by the slingshot
pings off of with a *thock*.
And he spins with the shock
and odd distance of it

from me—sorcery
it must be—and rushes
into the deeper bushes
and oncoming greenery,

then into the distances
the mountain gives,
where he lives
in such circumstances

as he must relearn
and will have to be,
again, even so hungry,
able to discern.

FIRST PERSON

One lies on one's back in the woods, savoring the sun,
and for some reason one has opted
for what Fowler calls the "false first person pronoun"—one,
that is, over the other. One brushes an ant from one's ear.
One peers up into the breeze-swayed branches
of a ponderosa pine, one among many
one has arranged oneself under. Perhaps the wind,
which is easy and warm, dislodged the ant
one swept from one's ear, meaning
it had fallen many times its height to land there,
in the whorl of the ear of one. In truth, one wishes
for the tongue of a sylph instead of an ant. Even two sylphs,
one thinks, though perhaps it is not sylphs one means—
they being invisible spirits of the air—
but rather the slender girls of one's conjuring. (One conjures,
one admits.) Thinking one dead, a deer approaches.
One imagines being a deer, but then one rises
to a seated position, so that the deer will startle
and run. If only one could run as a deer does.
If one were not so weary, one would that very deer chase
a ways, beguiled by the wave of its white tail.
But no, one is molten. One seems to have no bones.
One shall not run, not now, nor even rise.
Instead, one shall subside to one's supine pose
and by the sun through the needles of the trees be dappled.
Though of course one should avoid the word *dappled*.
One knows this. Yet something about the sun
and the sway of the shadows makes one
larcenous as well as slothful. And as one acknowledges

one's Hopkinsian trespass, one notes
perhaps the same sort of finch spoken of
in his poem and sees one's borrowing as praise.
Of the finch, that is, although it dawns on one
that this particular finch is an American goldfinch,
and one decides one's praise is for him instead, the poet.
One feels literary and allusive then. It seems one's time
upon one's back in the woods is not wasted after all.
There is the *squeegee-squeegee-squeegee-squeegee* song
of the goldfinch. One is delighted by the nineteen *ees*
in the preceding line, not one of which has been written,
since one is reclined under the trees
with none of the usual writing implements. (One counts them
in one's head and upon one's fingers instead.) One's 1965
Book-of-the-Month Club edition of Fowler's *Modern*
English Usage delights one also, though it is a quarter mile away
and stamped with the name and address of a dead woman
one knew once. One knew her and she died, and one is glad
to have known her, for she was droll and brilliant,
although one wishes one had known her when she was young.
Once one was young but is no longer,
though one still conjures as if one were—sylphs, women,
the too-soon dead, the chaste and priestly poets of yore.
Otherwise, one does not imagine one is certain of much.
In fact, one is almost asleep, but then a hawk alights
on the limb directly above, a rabbit in its talons.
One's breath is held. One perceives the soul
of the rabbit does not abide. One dares not move,
even though one's face and white T-shirt

will soon be dappled with the rabbit's blood.
One imagines. One thinks of the one one loves
and knows that she will startle
to see one's bloody face and shirt.
One will stand seemingly wounded and speak to her
of wind and sun, the hawk and its prey, the finch and the deer,
even Fowler (all things whose beauty is past change),
and the one one loves will not understand at first
when one insists that one must never be
the last one
to die.

KONG

The new porch light casts a much brighter glow
and an immense, probably sixty-foot-long shadow
of me out beyond the woodshed, where I'm bound.

And everyone knows, having learned the mechanics
of shadows in childhood, that with each step I take
away from the light, the shadow grows even larger,

though fainter and therefore less impressive.
I like to watch the darkest version of myself stacking
stove logs in the rack, each one the bulk

of a steer, and adding them to a truck-sized black rectangle
attached to the infinite darkness of the house.
Or of its shadow, at least. And when I walk

empty-handed back to the shed, I peer into that dark
and see, thrown across the snow, a bright trapezoid of gold
from the bedroom window, where your own shadow

undresses for bed, much larger than in real life, it's true,
but still too small for one so titanic as I have become.
Soon, however, I will return to the house, turn off

the porch light, stuff three or four logs in the stove,
and enter the bedroom then lit only by our two small
bedside lamps, hardly casting shadows at all.

He must have known the feeling, Jack Driscoll,
first mate of the SS *Venture*, with whom Ann Darrow
had fallen in love on the way to the island,

before Kong, before his enormous, expressive eyes
and his very black and gentle hands had held her
a quarter mile in the air over Manhattan.

It would never have left him, that feeling,
for all the years of their lives together, as she peered,
just like you do, into his sad, inadequate gaze.

CARHOPS, WITH LARKIN

1

Those were the days of sleeker deliveries,
blonde idealism, Marilyn in the moon.
In the town I grew up in, some dozen
burgeries featured them, wielding trays

sometimes as teeteringly stacked
as were their deliverers, whom the bosses knew
would draw as many customers as the food—
and no doubt they did—although looking back

I loved the food too, the ground beasts
and cheese, the abundantly salted fries,
the tiny plastic bowls of coleslaw
there beneath the lights, on trays where rested

also the frosted, sweaty mugs of root beer.
And if things were slow, an actual girl
might linger for a minute and converse,
banter, or tease, until over there

some brighter car or handsomer, older guy
pulled in. They carried at their waists
dispensers and repositories of change
that jingled when they went away.

2

They're still around, here and there,
though some are boys, like tonight's,
who calls me "sir," a label itself archaic,
all that sixty-year-old music in the air.

Larkin's sitting next to me, long-gone
Philip, eyeing the girls and feeling bitter
about the boy and wishing for a warm beer.
"Mightn't a chap just ask for that redheaded one?"

he asks. And I confess it's my fault.
I should have picked a different slot.
But then he sees, from his seat
on the passenger side, a leggy brunette

haul a burdened tray to the car next door
and reaches out a pale, ghostly hand
to pat her ass, and fails, then sighs. "I can't stand
being dead," he says, trying to be here

but being nowhere. Then he asks, "Have any luck
with one of these in your day, then?"
Now we're talking. There were some, back when,
who'd hop in back and fuck and fuck

you up in turn. He winces at the allusion.
Everything grows farther away:
carhops, the moon, parents, night. It's strange;
the carhop turns and screams through my illusion.

EARTHQUAKE LIGHT

grounds us [handwritten]

1.   *March 11, 2011*   *fact* [handwritten]

The ANS mind + the hen's one the same mind: full engagement [handwritten, top right]

2.   Earlier tonight an owl nailed the insomniac white hen.
She'd fluttered up onto a fence post to peer at the moonlight,
to meditate in her usual way on the sadness of the world   *= wonderful* [handwritten]

and perhaps the hundreds of vanished eggs of her long life here.
I was watching from the porch and thinking she ought not to be
where she was, and then she wasn't, but taken up, a white hankie

diminishing in the east, one the owl would not ever drop.
Now an hour after, the new night wind spins up a leghorn ghost
of her fallen feathers, under the moon and along the meadow grass.

Corpse candle, friar's lantern, will-o'-the-wisp chicken soul
dragging its way toward me, that I might acknowledge her loss
and her generosity, and wonder again about her long-standing

— could've stopped here / but downshifted again, kept going [handwritten]

inability to sleep on certain nights. There are sky lights
beyond our understanding and dogs whose work it is to scent
the cancer no instrument can see. On the nights she could not sleep,

the hen Cassandra Blue perched herself with a clear view to the west
and studied the sky, every two seconds canting her head a few degrees
one way or the other. What she saw or if she saw it I cannot say,

pulls back, another observed fact [handwritten]

29

though it seemed that something, always, somewhere, was about to go
terribly wrong. Then again, it always is. Now there's a swirl
of wind in the meadow, spinning three or four final white feathers

west to east across it, and there's a coyote come foolishly out
into the open, hypnotized by feather flicker, or scent, then seeing
by moonlight the too-blue shimmer of my eyes, and running for its life.

TIMEX

Freeing a crossways stob of fractured pine, perhaps,
the man who'd saved himself one trip down the ladder
to the off switch and still another one back up,
and who'd saved himself that same trip so often
he was proud of the vertical miles unclimbed
and undescended, and the sweat from them he had not sweated,

but this time, by some slip or somehow-too-far stretch, he fell
straight down the slick steel throat of the wood chipper
headfirst, taking whatever had stopped it with him
and vanishing in an instantaneous blat and a ghost
of blood vapor, becoming, like that, a pile of human pulp
in the half-full trailer of a chip truck scheduled in fifteen minutes

for the mill. Or so it was theorized by company investigators
and a man sent from the office of occupational safety,
whose suggestion that an off switch might be installed
at the top of the platform as well as the bottom
was implemented, though not mentioned in the final report
or in the newspaper. The one whose pages were made

from pulp that might have, despite the long boil
and bleaching process, contained some rendered human element
as well, although the paper also went on at length to describe
the company's generous settlement, not required, given the cause
was worker avoidance of corporate safety regulations.
No word, however, on whose job it must have been

to recover what could be of the body in the trailer.
Supple bone shards, mostly, unidentifiable nodules
of tissue, three swatches of scalp still haired. They were a man
and a woman, two employees of the state department of health,
one of whom also retrieved, with tweezers, and offered
to the victim's wife, the minute hand from his watch.

PART TWO

POSSIBLES

DESCARTES

September 2010

The aggravation of reading philosophy
to fall asleep is that you can only sleep
while reading. Once you turn out the light,
you're awake again, swamped in conundrums
and that elaborate subordinating syntax
with which the fact of your own existence
is made debatable. I read Descartes,
therefore I am sleepy. I sleep not,
therefore I think and am desperate not to.
As for the moon, unless my senses deceive me,
it is full, and though the pull of it provides for the tides,
there's no surf thrash here to lull me asleep. Instead,
I keep thinking of Francine, Descartes's daughter,
who died at five of scarlet fever.
The brightness of the moon allows me
to study the blood in my eyelids,
which I am otherwise uncertain is truly there.
Not even thinking about it proves it,
although, if Descartes was correct, thinking suggests
that I am, as he must have been,
susceptible to what is called heartbreak,
a metaphorical rendering of grief.
It would have kept him awake too,
370 years ago this month.
After her passing, it took him two years
to demonstrate, at last, the immortality
of the human soul, and still she was gone,

and still I cannot sleep for thinking.
The impossible to be borne is withstood,
and philosophy is nothing
the metaphorical heart cannot annihilate.
Little about the moon has changed
since Descartes would have looked upon it and thought,
though he must have also felt how little his thinking mattered
in the end, proving, as it did, nothing but that she had been,
and was, though he could not stop thinking of her, no more.

DADA DOODADS

The house the widow sold us
contained, she said, an attic full of treasure
or trash, and it would be our adventure,
my wife's and mine, to discover which.

And what it was, was a museum, a gallery,
or at the very least a monument
to the organizational skills of her late husband,
a veteran of World War I, dead many years.

Everything boxed, stacked, and labeled,
and every label gospel. "Two '37 Ford
hubcaps, one dented," and inside,
just that. "Shells from the beach, Atlantic,"

another from the Pacific. Old dishes,
so noted. A box of paper bags, another
of boxes. A box of "brown work pants,
never worn." Another at the bottom

of a tall stack, "Assorted screws," weighed
fifty pounds. And I, being less afraid
of spiders than my wife, was appointed auditor,
and found only accuracy and doodads:

there was a box in which I discovered—
I counted them—"fifty-four things
of no apparent use," exactly as he'd said,
and I worked my way from the attic's far end

to the one nearest the trapdoor back down
into the bedroom closet, stretching out
to take up from the decades' accumulated dust
the final container of more than a hundred

I investigated there. In his usual
block-print letters, the following:
"Empty box"—which a first shake
seemed to confirm as true, but still

I looked inside to be sure. And may I say
how glad I was then, that by some dumb luck
I had begun my accounting,
as he must have wished someone to,

at that far, other end. And may
I also say how much my respect for him,
or her, as well as my compassion—
for her, for him, for all the world—

was increased at just that moment,
since this last box contained only,
in the same black marker, scrawled diagonally
across the bottom, the word *nothing*.

FOR I WILL CONSIDER MY CAT LENORE

For she has, in this her twelfth year of hunting,
lost some weight in the summer, despite
the daily, even hourly, slaughter of everything
smaller than she and unable to escape her.
For she had for some time, unbeknownst to me,
relieved herself on my favorite dress shoes,
making them foul and fit only for the fire.
For though she be named after the place
she was born, as long as such legions as she requires
might be dispatched and often devoured
in whole or part, she is happy to be here
or there, it hardly matters otherwise.
For she does not like me, and I know not why,
and offer her each morning a tablespoon of cream,
which she will deign to lap a bit, then abandon
to the dog. For there is her purr
in the lap of my daughter, whose cat she was,
and there is her purr in the laps of my sons
and my friends, though her purr
in the lap of he who offers her cream
whirreth never. For the practical worth of her depredations
is the ratio by which those preyed upon
enter not the house. For the house is in the woods
and the woods are also full of those whose depredations
upon her are as avidly sought as hers upon her prey.
For she is luckier than her mother
and brother, gotten by owl, coyotes, or eagle,
or perhaps even one of those of the same order as she:
bobcat, lion, or lynx. For she is gray

and invisible, it seems. For she cougheth up
elaborate balls of her own fur upon the carpet
for me. For I have labored to love her
and have accomplished by such labors
an understanding, at least, since I have watched her
at the hunt and been inspired by the single-mindedness
and excellence of her predatory disposition.
For I have also wondered what manner of attentiveness
of my own I might have brought to bear
upon anything that could equal hers,
unless it be praise. For the sun and the moon,
for the plenitude of mice, and for the still-beautiful
back of the hummingbird she has left in the ashtray,
next to the chair on the porch of my shack.
For it is a calliope hummingbird,
smaller than my little finger, and its purple cowl,
in the time I have attended to this consideration
of its killer, has, without my notice, faded,
and Lenore herself has uncoiled from the chair
where she had slept for more than an hour,
and walked back into the woods,
to which I will toss
the hummingbird's almost weightless body,
which she left me, so that I might feel
exactly the way I do right now.

The birdhouse made from a gourd is wired
to a flanged loop of steel and screwed to the southeast post
of the shack. Two holes at the top—near where the stem was,
for a thong of leather to hang it by, which broke long ago—
are now the finger holes of the mournful wind instrument it's become.
The broad, round bowl of it makes a sort of birdly
basso profundo that pearls through the steel, into the post,
into the floor joists and walls, in two notes: a slightly sharp D
and an equally sharp F, says the guitar tuner,
which explains why all my thinking these days
is in B-flat, a difficult key for all but the clarinet
and this sudden covey of nuthatches, whose collective woe
makes it a minor chord I am in the middle of.
Nothing to do but hoist such silks as the luff
of limbs and needles suggests, and sail on,
the barely-escaped-from-the-cat chipmunk chattering
like a gull, and the mountain's last drift of snow
resembling the back of a sounding whale. Hear the thrum of the rigging,
Daggoo? Hear its profoundest woo, its sensible gobbledy-goo
and doo-wop, the boo-hoos of the spheres, by vectors and veers,
by tacks and refractal jabberings, taking us deeper into the weirdness
of the ghost sea those prairie hills were the bottom of once,
this nowhere we shall not be returning from.
Draw the lines! Assume the crow's nest, Pip. This ship
sails on music and wind, and away with birds.

NIGHTINGALE CAPABILITY

Italy, May 2011

We've been in Bogliasco a week
before we understand the bird that's wakened us
each miserably early morning is a nightingale.

I am pleased by this, just as I was years ago,
when I had my picture taken in Rome,
kneeling next to the gravestone of John Keats.

Every time I look at that picture, I think, *There I am, kneeling
next to the gravestone of John Keats*. And this week,
wakened every dark morning before four, I think,

I'm hearing the same kind of bird Keats wrote of, at Hampstead,
in one of the great odes of 1819, and it makes me a little sad
to confess that of them all I love the nightingale ode least.

Even the bird's singing—fulsome and musical,
especially in the still-dark Ligurian morning—
does not appeal to me as it did to Keats. At this deep blue

and aubadial hour, it's too loud. And too much.
But then, so is the fact that on Bartleby.com,
right there on my screen next to Keats's poem,

is Alexia. She's beautiful and pouty, barely dressed,
"in a relationship," it says in Italian, but who
"ha insoddisfatti desideri." She has "unsatisfied desires,"

in other words. *"Aiutala!"* it implores. Help her! Too much, yes,
but interesting: Keats, a nightingale, unsatisfied desires,
the longing for perfection, and Alexia. Here she is again,

this time alongside "To Autumn," a poem I prefer,
although now I'm puzzled by both her abundance
and her ubiquity, since she's next to the "Grecian Urn"

and "Melancholy" too. She's *not* by the "Ode to Psyche,"
which is strange, since the first words of that one are
"O Goddess!" and clearly that's what Alexia's meant to appear

to anyone who comes upon her here. (She's thirty-four, it says,
almost a decade older than Keats ever was.)
For some reason Bartleby prefers not to offer "Indolence" at all;

it's nowhere on the site, though Keats himself described its subject
as "the only happiness . . . the body overpowering the Mind,"
something Alexia could be said to personify: a bold lover

one can never kiss. As for the figures on the urn, it's true
they will live in supple youth and mad pursuit
as long as does the urn, and their desires will

in all that time go unsatisfied: boughs that cannot shed
their leaves, the piper who, unwearied, pipes new songs forever,
the figures forever warm and still to be enjoyed, forever

panting, forever young. Some believe Keats died a virgin.
Others think his most worldly friend, Brown,
surely took him to a brothel once. Meanwhile, here in the dark

Italian morning, I left the woman I love in bed a floor below
in order to investigate a bird whose song I never heard
except in words. I made my way to where, thousands of miles

from home and all my books, I could examine
how such a thing might matter to me. And when I sought
Keats's poems electronically, there was Alexia,

and since then I have thought more of her than of Keats,
or my beloved, or the nightingale still singing outside.
Even leaning dangerously far out the studio window,

I can't see it. And back on the computer screen, Alexia—
despite the almost two-centuries-old, deathless lines
to her right—insists that it is she who should have my attention,

even as the nightingale sings on. Of love,
Keats said, "It is my religion. I could die for it."
He also said, "I would sooner fail than not be among

the greatest," and then he died, believing himself a failure.
If I abandon this task soon and return to our room,
I'll find my lover in bed, sleep-warm and soft. But still,

there remains something I have not said and believed I could.
I thought it had to do with poetry, but it seems I was wrong.
Keats's desire was to make something beautiful and true,

to feel the satisfaction not only of knowing he'd done so,
but to believe that the world would see it and acknowledge it too.
And still, that acknowledgment came too late to do him any good.

One more, and among the least, in the endless human plague
of unsatisfied desires. And what I might have said, or might yet,
has little to do with the viewless wings of Poesy,

and more to do with the way the dull brain perplexes and retards
the body's progress toward love. Imagine writing the line,
"More happy love! more happy, happy love!" What does it mean

that I can't? Her lack of satisfaction makes Alexia look miserable
in an ever-so-ravishable way, but if I clicked on *"Aiutala,"*
I would be no closer to her than I am to Keats.

Therefore, the villa's twenty-four stone stairs
back down to the second floor fly by as swift as in a dream,
and when I'm back in my bed and my lover's arms again,

it is my mind that reawakens and overpowers, for a while at least,
my body, and I speak: nothing of Alexia, Keats, the nightingale, or the odes;
nothing of how tender the night has been, or the least sickness for home;

only remembrance, softly: that she recall the night of the day
she took my picture as I knelt by the grave of a Young English Poet.
Weary from hours walking the ancient streets of Rome,

we lay on a rooftop terrace no more than a hundred yards
from the room he died in. In the distance, St. Peter's dome
glowed silver-blue. Remember? We were there all night,

and all night, gulls from the Tiber passed overhead, squawking.
No one would ever describe their calls as soulful or melodious,
but that night, I say, they were beautiful, and she is satisfied.

CAREERS

Not a bonehead, though yes, we called
the class she was enrolled in that—those
of us who taught such classes, believing
that mucking among the illiterates was beneath us.
We were meant for finer things: the joys
of allusion and figure, the lushness that is literature.

And yet, for this assignment, the dreaded process
paper, for which I had encouraged them
to consider nothing too mundane or daily,
she had written—in contrast to her dreary
colleagues, the changers of oil and bakers of cookies—
a paper that, step-by-step, described

in impressive and vastly appealing detail
her morning shower. She was not guileless either.
She knew I could not—as I confronted
each paragraph's sequential topic sentence—
not imagine her there: first her hair, then her face,
then her body from her arms and shoulders to her waist,

and from her feet back up to what she called—
most fetchingly—her "possibles," which
by such mention she must have known those too
I could not possibly help but imagine. She finished
by shaving her underarms and her legs,
wrapping a towel around her, and combing out her hair.

O, let us learn, I thought to myself that day, humility
and all the humble pitfalls and perils of language
and instruction. If there were a career in bathing
and reporting the processes thereof, she was home free.
And there were jobs, I did not doubt, that her paper,
offered as a letter of application, might well land her,

if only she sat across the desk from someone
not at all like me and beamed the way she did,
mostly in pride. I struck three semicolons,
one of them used correctly but pointlessly.
She leaned in very close; she was not pleased
with her A-minus, but honestly thrilled.

I realized I was hardly older than she was,
but at the weekly meeting with my own colleagues
I did not speak of her at all, nor of the ballplayer
who'd threatened to break my nose if he did not pass,
nor of the tree-crushed, almost quadriplegic former logger
whose papers were transcribed by an amanuensis

of nearly intolerable linguistic ignorance. This would be
my life for some years. It was a way to live.
The girl aimed to be a nurse and marry a doctor.
The ballplayer went to the bigs and became
a millionaire. The hired scribe left the logger
in his motor-driven wheelchair on a dock by the river,

to fish, and somehow the motor joystick was nudged
just enough so that he tumbled in and drowned.
The scribe, from the office of occupational rehabilitation,
in an act supremely needless and disarming,
brought the logger's final paper to me
and wept in my office like a baby.

LEGEND

It is the legend, regarding the hole at the Big Eddy
of the Clearwater River, that it be not bottomless
but a might-as-well-be warren of shelves, caves,
and chambers, lost and cast-off sand and silt makings
so churned by the river's hydraulics that every depth-gauge
sinker has spun from it a wasted mile or two
of horizontal measurement that is never returned.

Which is why we have had to imagine,
these forty and more years after the incident, the three
witnesses now gone, how carefully
the doctor's wife must have driven the Cadillac down
the boat ramp and into the water, and how the car
strangely floated, turning slowly, sunk to the roofline,
until it vanished at what must have been the very mouth

of the myth of bottomlessness itself: one Coupe de Ville
Cadillac, 1963, yellow, windows according to witnesses
rolled up tight, and holding the driver, presumed to be
a twenty-nine-year-old mother of three children,
presumed also to have been inside. Such is the power
of plain police reportage, and also of the grappling hooks
that over the next week brought to the surface

twelve sunken logs and the carcass of a drowned moose,
before the search was abandoned and a service performed
on the beach there. Here is a black-and-white picture
of several hundred mourners. Late spring. The beach is pale sand,
and white shoes dangle from the fingers of several of the women.
From this angle, the highway roadbed looking down,
the river turns above the eddy like water in a drain.

Go down there now, in the turn of it, and see
the Cadillac descend among the many oscillating logs
untouched, scraping not the least outcropping and coming
at last to rest on an only slightly slanted shelf,
a right rear wheel over the edge and slowing
to a stop. By now the rubber window gaskets
will have disintegrated, and sometimes a sturgeon

longer than the Coupe de Ville itself
will slide its soft sucker mouth along a glassy seam
for no reason but the dim reminder of a soup
it sipped there once. Such is the power of memory,
which this is not. Not of the doctor's yellow Cadillac, nor
of his beautiful wife behind the wheel and headed out of town.
She looked your way, but you did not see her see you at all.

Some thug or other was always vanishing.
East St. Louis, my father said. He always said that.
City of my birth. The new highway made it possible
to pass the place by, ill-lit, seemingly unpeopled.
He drove fast. The windows were down.
He'd let me extend the blade of my hand
into the wind of our going, and we were passing
a large trailer-truck loaded with crushed,
compacted cars—a recognizable Chevrolet emblem
on one, and from another, a slip of fabric,
headliner or upholstery, black and pointed
at its end, resembling, I remember, a necktie.

THE HISTORY OF GODS

When a lesser species rises among them
to consume the sun immemorially theirs,
redwoods will sometimes let go a great limb

and crush the interloper where it stands,
implying intent and therefore what we know
as consciousness. It is theorized they may be able,

via their massive and elaborate root systems,
to command the groundwater itself, for the benefit
only of their kind—a government and fealty of trees.

Though perhaps what seems intentional
is simply part of the balance they exemplify,
the fallen limb afflicted by a disruption

in the nutrient flow precisely above where a hemlock
or pine has sprung forth, suggesting the decision
is no decision at all but simply cause and effect,

silvicultural machinery, as though it were not the mind
of a god but a body, reflexive to stimulus and wound,
actions neither revenge nor damnation nor self-preservation.

Although the darkness they rise from is their own creation,
and high in their canopies, lichens not found below,
delicate as fog, and birds that might as well be angels.

BABEL

The language he speaks and writes is spoken
and written by no one but him, which solves,
for him at least, the problem of audience.
Unless somehow, against the odds, he believes

there is someone to whom his alphabet speaks,
and his words—if they are words and not notes
of some other sort of singing, a system of clicks
and impossible vowels, the strange habitats

in which his bent and prickly syllables live.
The patience with which he clears his throat
and nods to us and begins, mild and tentative
at first, to read, or sing, or ceremonially recite

the epic of his people or the story of his God
or the description of his lost beloved's body,
moves us so each time, we concentrate and nod
but understand nothing at all of what he

has said. When he's finished, he looks at us
expectantly, and we, in our own inadequate tongues,
and often gesticulating wildly, discuss
the majesty of his accomplishment, which no one

fathoms any part of, least of all our praise,
if that's what it is, since we too are the last
or perhaps the only ones ever to raise
into the air such utterances—from the past

or the future or from this very moment in time,
when no one knows what anyone means to say or tell,
not even at night, when we seem to pray, then recline
on our bunks, each in his own terrible, familiar cell,

with the toilet and the night-light, with the reams
of paper, filled and yet to be, that surround us,
and he goes on speaking through our dreams,
where everything, making sense, astounds us.

The umbrellas misfired, the rain broke down,
all the seed-white dandelions were bludgeoned
to a fluffy paste. The bell tower ratcheted
up its terrible black birds. Negotiations
broke out between thunder and cell phones
despite the enormous vee of geese going by.
Someone whispered the secret of the match
to a cigarette, and hail commenced
machine-gunning a delicate wing of smoke.
Cruel world for bathing beauties, though. The clatter
of flip-flops rose like an ovation for the nation
of May, and the Goth boy in his black greatcoat
pale as the Jesus over Rio and similarly stanced,
having raised his arms and brought to the air
not only the wail of the noon whistle
but also the howl of a hound dog leashed to a hydrant,
as though it, in the midst of such majesty,
in the last week of classes, were his wolf.

PART THREE

DARK BLUE MOUTH

Kripalu

GOLDFINCHES

He could not, he insisted, take his eyes
from the pistol's muzzle, calculating
as he watched it, from the way it quivered—
and cocked, as it was, a single action,
it seemed—how easily that quivering
could cause it, without the man's intending,
to discharge, as we say, and thinking too,
given its angle, what part of him would,
in that event, be thus sundered and torn.
Although, this was after the fact, later,
as he explained to the two policemen,
how he kept his left hand in front of him,
as though he might catch the slug, or block it,
even as he reached slowly behind him
and produced, with thumb and index finger,
the wallet he dropped mildly between them
and stepped back from as the mugger stepped forward
and bent to retrieve it.
                              Only then
did he see not the pistol, but the tattoo
of the birds on the other's left forearm.
Sundered and torn, he'd said. Those were his words,
though the policeman writing it all down
did not write it all down that way, except
for the tattoo, its three colorful birds
and the leafy gray branch they perched upon.
Birds, he'd said, American goldfinches,
of the sort that winter in the canyons

east and south of the city, and which sing,
canary-like, *ti-dee-di-di*, sweetly,
and gather in flocks on winter mornings,
bobbing on the limbs of leafless birches,
to feed on the last dry catkins and fly
all at once, as one, with a single mind,
or none, startled by nothing, or by some move
nothing but one or all the birds could see.
Almost exactly life-size, and well done,
artistically, even, in the dim lights
of that backstreet he'd walked a thousand times.
Nicely rendered songbirds, he'd said, which were
how it was the culprit would be, as we say,
so easily apprehended, strung out,
asleep in an aging junker Plymouth
in the city's best park, the pistol snugged,
the newspaper reported, "like a teddy bear,
directly under the suspect's chin,
the victim's wallet still in his pocket."
It also spoke of the tattoo only
in the most general terms, as that which,
being the classic identifying mark,
along with the wallet, would convict him.
Still, thereafter, he, the victim, always
described the goldfinches in great detail,
feeling, as he'd come to, that it was they
who might well have saved him, remembering
how slowly he'd moved, so as not to startle

the birds outside his window, and not
to have to keep seeing, neither in memory
nor dream, the dark blue mouth of the pistol.

BLACKJACK

In fact, it's a beautiful thing: expertly made,
the egg of lead in the business end

and the flexible leather braid
leading to a bulb for the hand

and the loop for the jacker's wrist,
kinetic energy far superior to a fist's.

It is also perfect for holding a book
open to a certain page or passage.

How it feels about such work,
we cannot know but can imagine,

being men and wondering, after all—
the thud and crumple, the fall.

In the palm of my left hand, I slap it; then
he, in his right, my left-handed, bookish friend.

DELICIOUS

He loves how cold she always is. Even sandwiched
in their matched, fully-zipped-together sleeping bags,
she presses herself to his back, chilled tomato to the ham of him.

It's August, but the river runs an arm's length below them,
runs her height from them southwest, and it is cold, colder
than she is, though here is where she loves to sleep,

inside the almost-kiss of it, the river's endless consumption
of stones, its long nightly respirations risen into veils,
into vapor tatters a morning sun unwinds and licks away.

This is how it must be: her front sufficiently warmed, she turns
and he must also turn, the spoon of meat he is all night, and hot,
a film of almost-sweat across him like a condiment

she cannot get enough of. He is rich, he thinks. He is taste
and succulence. He is delicious. And if one bench of floodplain
farther up and away from where they lie would be warmer,

still he knows it would be too far, for her, from what she loves
as much as she loves his hands and chest, his salt-skin shoulders
and his breath: this river she cannot live without

for long. He does not mind such faithlessness as that.
She would be the trout she loves as much as she loves him,
so therefore he lives alongside the water, breathing with her also,

and when the sun at last clears the eastern ridge
and the dew from the tent's dome, like the river's mists,
is swallowed by the air, he like the mist rises,

pared away from her, and builds her
a small morning fire, and fires the water for coffee,
and is allowed, as the most modest recompense, to stand

and watch through the sliver of vent at the top of the tent door
as she rises too, bare and half warm, to dress again
for the day—the chilled breasts and backside

submerged inside her clothes as the trout is
in the river—for though he also loves the trout
and will be all the sun long troubled

by the difficulty of the lure, the fly, the hook that holds
inside what appetite any of them might imagine,
still he knows, come night, come the water's icy vapors

upward, that he will hold her as he might, lucky under the moon
and near the trout—its beautiful meat and bone, its edible skin—
where they sleep, on the round of the river's cold lip.

PN
Tender
, Accepting
, playful + respectful
, embraces this finds
the stamp
Beauty in it.

PN's capacity to
find beauty
in these
sad moments

SWEET MAGNET

It is the stage called "word salad,"
says the neurologist: schizophasia—
the patient's lexicon cut loose
from its roots, diced sometimes
into awkward syllables but assembled
into mostly recognizable syntax still.

(honest + understated)

Mostly I am uneasy, my father,
the patient, sitting between us,
my mother and me, and saying nothing
just now. True, he can't remember
where I live sometimes, and he wonders where
the babies are, meaning my sister and me.

When we've returned to his room,
my father contemplates the back of his hand
for a long time. Studies it, even, then says,
"No, I believe that moon is bullshit."
Then he looks at his palm, and beckons me
to come closer, so that I might hear

and understand. "It's presidential war,"
he says. "That's the way it's always been
with me. Toothpaste. The weather."
I agree. "Let's get the car and drive far,"
he says. "I loved that spaghetti necktie.
Nothing to any of it but missing drums."

65

Speak what you will. Each glossolalium
sings. At lunch the maraschino cherry
in his fruit cocktail is a sweet magnet,
the orderly's mop is mysterious silver,
and the slick of its wash across the floor
is something about the soul of a spoon.

ODE TO MY BOOTS

Long hooves removed, sweat-stewed
and leather-redolent. Foot hovels, laces
cross-hatched up the fronts, tag ends untied,
orphaned parentheses, speechless tongues,
heels and soles rounded by miles. Black eggs
from which pale birds have emerged
that step-by-step had flown wingless through the world
in them. The pale intermediaries, the socks,
fat woolen blossoms reborn as buds
in the pure soil of waiting in the drawer, sheaths
to be entered for the entering of the shaft,
into the supple vamp, to be embraced by the welt,
swaddled in the gussets and bound there.
And bound also into the world, which accepts
the boots as the boots accept the feet,
earth which accepts the prints of the boots
as the boots accept the prints the feet leave in them,
miles of motion memorialized as stillness.
My hand, reaching inside each boot,
reads the history of my walking there,
which is nowhere and anywhere:
ten tentacles of pivot and balance;
the two balls of power; the arches, synecdoches
of a million steps; and the heels of transition
and restraint. Fossils of perambulation,
life-and-death masks of departure and return,
blunt destinationless etchings of boot memory.
These shed, heavy husks: years in them,

though they have no notion
of where they have been, and where,
with luck, they may yet take me.

ON A SERIES OF FOUR PHOTOGRAPHS

As it would turn out, even under the weight of its considerable shell,
the snail ascended the wall of an enclosure made of razor blades
and slid across a battlement of seven honed edges on nothing

but its unmysterious, whisper-thin, moon-shimmer glister, a whisker
of which still sags in four of the six spaces between the blades
but sits like miniscule pearlescent and orbicular spittles atop

the glinty parapets themselves: see Figure 4, in which just the snail's tail
can be seen as it descends into the bowl of garden greens and radicchio
that will be its reward. Figure 1 is also nice: the gelatinous horns

cresting the castle wall; but Figures 2 and 3 comprise the point of it all:
the little guy scudding over the awful edges like a schooner cresting
waves, the canvas of his burled shell aflicker, suggesting great speed.

Before he dreamed of being the tree
he dreamed of being the owl.
Before he dreamed of being the owl
he dreamed of being the flicker.

Before he dreamed of being the flicker
he dreamed of being the buck.
But the buck ran away, and the flicker
flew, and the owl scuttled sideways

out of sight, and all that was left
was the tree he dreamed of being,
so he dreamed of being the tree.
He was sifting the sunlight and the light

breeze swaying his needles just enough.
He welcomed the owl and said good-bye
to the flicker and the buck. He waved
hello to the breeze and good-bye to it too.

He let a bundle of brown needles fall
and considered the man asleep at his foot.
The clouds going by could not distinguish him
from his brethren, and the ants

leaving his skin to wander the man's
could not distinguish the man from him,
but for maybe the warmth he also felt
enter him from the man's bark,

which was of a color much like his own.
He concluded that warmth was the by-product
of sleep, and he dreamed he was the man
asleep at his foot, dreaming of the buck,

and then the flicker, and then the owl,
before he remembered he was the tree,
dreaming of being the man, asleep,
dreaming of being the tree, dreaming.

CATECHISM

Next door the old pipe organ no longer wheezes.
Here, the new one's electric and hums.
Here, too, upholstered pews, a last-twice-as-long-as-Jesus
miracle fabric called Herculon, over foam the bums

of bums will appreciate. And me, sixteen,
sneaking out, faking a coughing spell,
and bound for the old church next door, alone,
but only for a while, I hope. The girl

I'm meeting there is named Babette, known as Butch.
Every Sunday for a month we've met there,
in the choir loft. She'll undress and let me watch,
and then we'll desanctify the place—the pews, the air,

the ashtray a former organist abandoned.
Afterward I'll light my Kool with hers.
The stained-glass window will be shot with sun
this morning and give our skins a special shimmer.

I almost believe I made this happen by praying,
every Sunday for half a year, alone and morose,
coming here and staying
until the doxology. Butch is pretty without her clothes.

If it is God from whom all blessings flow,
then what I've learned in the choir loft is faith.
Yes, she's there, and already naked by the time I show.
Holy, holy, holy, with her angelic mouth, she saith.

RUSH

The winter snow broke his arms.
He'd lost his hat and his head,
and I needed to rebuild him from
the mud up, and so unzipped his fly,

and there they were: a family
of mice nested in the crotch
of the pants that had once been mine,
a squirm of pink pods, two

of which tumbled out and down
onto the spring-warm ground
at our feet, and which I collected
and slipped carefully back in.

Then I zipped the fly again
and waited until today, a month
later in spring, the once fresh
bale of straw having sprouted green.

And yes, they're gone now,
all but the one whose foot it seemed
I'd caught, pulling the zipper up,
dun as a dry bean, mummified

in the sepulchre of my former pants.
I leave the fly closed this time,
and the mouse carcass breaks loose
and vanishes down a leg

as I jam more and more straw
down the waist hole to rebuild him,
the scarecrow I used to call Steve,
a name my wife, back in the years

of our courtship, had bestowed upon
that flesh of mine that had once
lived also in those parts of those pants.
Steve loved Diane in those days.

Now there's a spiffy belt of red
baling twine, a farmerly blue work shirt,
and somewhere down around his ankle
a spot of gone meat, like a tumor

or a lost, desiccate, misbegotten testicle
I hope the ants will feast upon.
This spring I give him a face as well,
a Halloween mask of my son's

from a few years back—a radio talk-show
blabbermouth—topped by the two-foot
conical dunce cap of a highway hazard
marker. Call it a cautionary tale, then:

seemingly happy in my pants, with a plastic face,
brainless, unable to dance, left arm
raised in a fist of straw, blessedly silent,
the scarecrow, nutless, with his new name.

"AMERICAN ARCHANGEL"

—Anne Sexton

Having licked the birdbath dry, the moose lies down
on the path to the front door: *Alces alces phlegmatica.*
Photographable through the kitchen window, he cranes
his broad neck westward for a nibble of autumn's wild strawberry
leaves. He won't leave until he's ready, and he's not.

I am, I have been made to know, too interested in him.
He's not an idea but a thing that shits thoughtlessly
and in prodigious abundance wherever he wants, and he wants
this morning, despite the dog's incessant barking—not at the sight
of him but at his half-ton scent—to rest. Therefore he rests.

And therefore I, sequestered by his rest, rest myself
in the bastion of my measly consequence, a consequence
of his immensity, his territorial instinct, and his thirst.
For every evening, on this, the dry side of the mountain,
I fill the birdbath, and every morning he drinks it dry.

Maybe what interests me is less moose than bird, a nuthatch
that landed on the rim of the bath as he lapped,
and drank its fill as well, flying away only
when he lifted his massive muzzle and inclined his deep
black sniffers its way, meaning, it seemed, no harm.

I have seen the disembowelments of the peaceable kingdom.
I've sawn a moose rack from the winter-killed head of one of his kind,
having scared off a pack of coyotes in the process.

I've rescued a nuthatch from the jaws of my own cat,
and now I'm imprisoned in my house by the presence of a moose.

Though not for long. He's rising, unwinding his long legs
and standing, stretching, shitting a peck of steaming bales.
The bowl of the birdbath is dry but cool, I suppose,
so he licks at it again, as though it is the blue itself
he means to consume, or the rime of its mineral deposits.

I cannot imagine, I confess, being uninterested in him.
His dewlap sways, he twitches his side-skin at an itch,
he heaves a gigantic breath and begins to move away,
and it may be he is no blessing upon me. It may be
there is no reason to speak of him at all.

THE ART OF EXCAVATION

The two-fingered sweep method works best,
brushing aside the needle thatch and duff
and exposing in the process more needle thatch
and duff. Although needle thatch and duff
sounds like a firm of British barristers,
and I am pleased already with my digging.

Like me, the ground here is undisturbed,
just as most memories are. Remembering nothing
I ever wrote or drew, I remember nevertheless
the flush of seeming wealth a Big Chief tablet
gave me: virginal; bold, broad lines and page-wide,
hyphenated intermediary ones the humps

of aitches and kickstands of arrs nudged against
and slanted from. Nary a thing to say nor a thought
to render unto ideaness, though: the expanse of the page
was a taunt this swath of nest-makings resembles
not at all. First of all, there are these calcite knuckles
of snails I uncover, little whorls aspiring to fossils.

Then a bone sliver, a tooth. In truth, such treasures
are everywhere, for soil is bone as much as bone is.
Here's a speckled fleck of eggshell and a diminutive knot
of pine resembling the profile of a failed president.
Here's a feather tip stiff as a beached fin.
Here's a button I'll take home and add to the box.

(In the households of the wealthy, do such boxes
exist? Admirals' brass, ambassadorial pearl?)
It was white once, this one. Now it's the color
of tea with cream. But wait. Here's another,
a deeper brown but otherwise identical. There's a story
here: she took the plackets and flung them wide,

Amanda, the beautiful daughter of the mountain recluse,
having her way with Pete, the mule skinner;
or maybe it was Clifton, chasing a wounded buck,
his right sleeve hung on a stob as he ripped them free.
No, wait: I'm missing Amanda. But then, here's
the gleaming black toe from a deer's hoof, then at last

a pale, translucent root the color of semen
and hairless as a worm, which, the mind wandering
as it does at such an enterprise, I begin to unearth
as carefully as an archaeologist uncovers a mandible.
It stretches, at a more or less constant depth
of six inches, almost the length of my leg

to a bulbous, pithy, empurpled tumor
the size of a softball, from which a single stem
rises to the withered, desiccate blossom of a trillium.
It's a root gall, a mass of scar tissue become
the individual itself, little pine forest Ahab face
wounded into being but bearing into the world

nevertheless its flower. And here's the click
of the black beetle crawling from under it,
wondering what's become of his roof,
and there's the clang of the triangle my wife uses
to call me back from wherever it is I've gotten to,
as per our arrangement: that I might return

from my daily quest and reload the wood crib
or sweep the spring-fallen pine needles
from the porch, that I might become a productive man
again, and not the sort who moseys through the woods
or sits on his ass, probing the ground for nothing,
although the buttons and the tooth are just what I need.

PART FOUR

PINIONED HEART IN THE HEAT OF IT

SOCIALISTS

Because he paid me union scale, I loved Christ
Schuler and monkeyed iron and copper water pipes
with his daughter, Katie O'Hare—KO, he called her,
and she was that, although she also liked to fight.
Not wrestle—which, when I could get ahold of her,
we would—but punch, kick, gouge, and bite. I mooned
over her teeth marks on my right shoulder for hours
one night, but no matter how I contrived
to contort my neck and stretch out my tongue,
I could not lick them as I wished. Nor her,
neither pugilistically speaking or otherwise.

"You keep that pipe of yours away from my daughter
or I'll torque the thing clean off with this wrench,"
Christ said, brandishing a fourteen-inch quick fit
my way. Then he laughed. "She's a sweet dumplin',
ain't she?" On the door of his truck, "Christ's Plumbing:
Just Like Jesus Would Do," the tailgate and bumper
festooned with stickers extolling the wisdom of Eugene V. Debs,
Norman Thomas, Albert Einstein, and Woody Guthrie.
"KO's hair's as red as America'll be someday," he said.

In every crawl space or basement, in some hidden spot
no owner or landlord would ever be likely to see,
he scrawled with a greasepaint pen the same slogan:
When the people shall have nothing more to eat,
they will eat the rich. And though I knew
he meant the moneyed ones whose places we worked on,
I confess the line's Rousseauian prognostication

was lost on me. All I wanted was to eat his sweet dumplin' up.
She taunted me, as we hefted eight-foot iron
sewer pipes, debating the vileness of capitalist shit,

and as she was indoctrinated by Christ, so by she was I.
Come July I'd have made an incision in the gut
of any plutocrat she'd aimed me toward, pulled loose
a loop of intestine, and fed it to a hungry dog for her.
And if she believed my conversion was not quite true,
it was Christ himself who convinced her otherwise,
saying over lunch his admiration for my grandfather,
an International Worker of the World and doomed
unionless coal miner dying even then of black lung.
In the face of his praise I looked at KO and she was smiling.

Which was how it came to be we came to be
naked in the crawl space of a seedy complex
of subsidized housing some shyster city father
was paying us to plumb on the cheap. The freckles
on her chest ended where the sun never shined,
but I counted every one like a vote and felt
as though it were not only Christ I was betraying
but somehow my grandfather too,
believing the things she'd told me for reasons
having little to do with the downtrodden masses

but, rather, that right before my eyes was her pale,
unfreckled, and delectable ass, as she fed
a length of second-rate copper water pipe up a hole

between the floor joists and wiggled at me,
then giggled. She'd be almost as old as I am today,
if she had not vanished one morning on the way to school.
They found her stripped, bound in baling twine,
face up in a pond on the outskirts of town.
Christ retired then and died a few years later,
my grandmother insisted, of a broken heart.

Katie O'Hare of the red, red hair, of the wedge
of neckline and shoulder freckles, daughter of Christ,
I loved you too, girl. The general theory was, you were
too beautiful for an unknown monster to resist.
The lesser thought was fascists, or some midwestern,
right-wing, anticommunist, self-appointed death squad
come to avenge your father's un-American tailgate philosophy.
Forgive me, if I find this latter take unlikely.

But you should also know, that among the pipes and faucets,
the toilets and showers of my hanging-by-its-fingertips
middle-class, mostly mortgaged American home,
I do not see or hear the water issue forth or vanish
without some thought of you and of your father.
He would not recognize the nation of your birth.
You fought hard, I'm sure, but your father
had no country to fight for. Only the earth.
He was, as you were, as I may be myself,
someday, a citizen of the world.

The intelligence of the birds had always pleased him.
Magpies and ravens, mostly—how they flew
along with the tractor, or lined the way
to the boneyard like watchers at a parade,
the tractor rocking under its bucket-load.
But the old mule was too big for the bucket;
so big, in fact, that he was sure, were he to fall it
where it stood, the tractor could not
drag the beast in chains all the way there.
So he haltered it and led it, three or four steps
at a time, over much of an autumn afternoon,
to the half-filled ravine's lip. And he understood
that it must have been the tractor that drew the birds,
for none were there, as he stroked
the lathered neck and withers, and whispered
his gratitude and consolation,
then nestled the muzzle of the .45 behind an ear
and turned his face away and tumbled it—
he never called it anything but mule—into a gash in the earth.
Smell of cordite then. Smell of dust. The mule
came to rest among the years-woven nest of bones
exactly on its back, a posture he knew
the coyotes would appreciate. He also knew their howls
as early as this evening might be heard,
and as with the already arriving magpies and ravens,
passing overhead as he walked back to the farm,
this too, in his sadness, pleased him.

"Disensouled," he said, and a chill
came over me, until I realized
he meant only that the wreck I'd been inspecting
had already been purchased. They were all

wrecks. It was a junkyard, after all.
I was looking for one the transmission,
transfer case, and rear differential
might be removed from and transplanted,

although what drew me to this one
was the shape of its wreckage: bashed
perpendicularly by a tree, U-shaped down
to the frame. But what had caught my eye

and held it was the flattened bench of the seat
stained almost entirely a deep ocherous brown.
"Them people never knew what hit 'em,"
he said. "Tree come down on the highway."

He shuffled his toothpick from the left
side of his mouth to the right. "Act of God."
There was a rig down the way a bit
he said I ought to see. "Other way around,

this one," he said. "Truck hit the tree."
The impact, far to the right, blew the engine
due left and broke the bellhousing off,
but the drivetrain looked solid and sound.

"Lookit there," he said. A perfect half-orb
blasted into the safety glass of the windshield.
"Fella's head," he said, working around it,
as he wrote on the windshield, "Sold."

"AIN'T NO USE"

Sarah Vaughan, 1959

As I listen, I like to imagine her
at Mister Kelly's in Chicago,
every man in the place aware
no one's ever sung the song so,

nor so perfectly. And by that perfection
is the wound at the source of it
turned salt within the wound it inflicts back,
the long-held vibratos felt

in the tongue and every other elsewhere
another tongue might have been.
Look at her. She's up there
in the lights and smoke. Sweets Edison's

indeeding and amening *chumps*
and true *fools* through the mute
of his I-am-right-next-to-her trumpet
and tells them all she don't give a hoot

if she ever hears your name again.
There is no part of her body not
singing now, not a single blessed thing
among the tenderest and most powerful parts

of who she is inside it, inside the skin,
under the dress and the lights, in the building

on Rush Street, under Chicago's wind
and a few city stars hardly showing.

It's also me she's singing to, I imagine.
The recording's fifty years old, but oh, how
she sings, there in Mister Kelly's establishment,
although the building is a steakhouse now.

They're from southern California or Texas,
a couple from actual Dixie-like places
with good barbecue, cockroaches, and humidity.
They're almost used to snow, come February.
Today, however, is a whiteout.
We gather at the tall windows and cannot see
the familiar secretary across the way, rolling a rock of type
up the mountain of her screen, nor the courtyard, its picnic table
resembling a snow-covered car. And still
the sun not only beams down through it all,
it's also made an arc of light across the sky above us,
a snowbow—shimmering, electric, and magnificent.
I can hardly get them to return to their desks
and the task at hand, a poem by Edwin Arlington Robinson,
who, being from Maine, knew a few things about snow,
and to whom the last soul standing at the window bears,
though he does not know it, a remarkable resemblance:
hair slicked from a part down the middle of his head,
gold-rimmed glasses, and a mustache
the size of a bratwurst waxed into points
on either side of his pale, bereaved-looking face.
They've never seen anything like it, the snowbow, I mean,
and mustachioed Corey—the student at the window,
from Baton Rouge—is still standing there
when Margo—she of the blue hair and tattoos,
a girl from the Montana Hi-Line—turns to him.
She's intense, her fairly new tongue stud sometimes clicks
against the back of her teeth when she's excited.
She takes his right hand in both of hers

and startles him from his reverie. And there they are,
silhouetted against the blowing snow, Corey
looking down and seeing in Margo's eyes
the same amazing thing he could not turn away from,
until he does and returns to his chair. We would tell you,
if we knew, the story that will unfold from them,
the many ways we cannot see, of which this
is the least, having to do not with the snow
or the light but what even they themselves could not know,
that he would break her heart repeatedly.

STOP AND LISTEN

Sometimes the woods at night are so still
the sound of your own breath
abashes you, to say nothing
of the racket as you walk.

Sometimes talking helps, saying
a poem, or even, if you're going downhill,
singing. Other times there's nothing
to do but stop and listen, or even sit

and close your eyes in the name
of attentiveness. In daylight,
there are birds, and for some reason
the wind too is always awake,

delivering weather or dust.
At night, you concentrate,
your listening is enhanced,
and sooner or later you will hear

a scale of bark let loose from a tree
or a needle tick from limb to limb
on its enormous journey to the earth.
And sometimes, having resumed

your walk, you will stop at the top
of the ridge above your house.
Its window lights will illumine the ground
around it, and you will listen again

and hear the faint hum of it—
the buzz of its lightbulbs, the industry
of its clocks. And sometimes
you will approach it as would a thief

and peer through the windows,
in order that you might covet,
being part of the world's greater silence,
everything that is already yours.

CALENDAR

I wish the month had one more day, or even two,
or that, in truth, I might live it again, if only
so that Lola might be with me a little while longer.

Not that the month has been anything special
in regards to her. Most of it I spent
away, and even the time with her,

in the light of her devastating, sultry gaze,
the fabulous black teddy, the sheer pink
negligee, the one visible garter snap,

the black hose, the carmine garter belt itself,
and the high-heeled pink mules, to say nothing
of the way she is seated on the golden

sheen of the love seat, or the way the right
cup of the teddy creates the most perfect
ripple of flesh at the side of the breast

it lifts just enough to cast a slender shadow
between it and the other one, nor even
the way her left leg is tucked under the right

thigh or the way she holds the heel of that mule
in her right hand as though bracing herself
against herself. Even in all this glory,

the time I spent with her consisted of nothing
more than the occasional glance
until today. Tomorrow I'll move on

to the beauty of next month, which, like every one
but this one, is nameless in a special way.
Four weeks ago, Firebelle; tomorrow, A Warm Welcome.

But today, dark already at four-thirty in the afternoon,
a snowstorm blowing in, it is Wednesday,
the thirtieth of Lola, 2011.

THE SCHOLAR

We were to know we would never know
as much about it as he did. He knew
we didn't care and believed his knowing
was evidence. He was a scholar,
a critic, a wielder of wit for it,
its minutiae and mysteries,
which for him were no mystery at all.
Machinery, maybe. Cogs and pistons,
the pinioned heart in the heat of it.
Someone asked about love, the fool.
Our backs ached. The sun was relentless.
He leaned on his hoe as though
it were a podium, drew a kerchief
from his pocket and wiped his face.
He pointed at the sky, where a hawk hovered,
awaiting the mouse that would bolt
from our work. One mouse was just
like another, and we were more or less
the same, except for what we'd never know,
which we knew, even without his saying so.

ANNA KARENINA

The inquisitive look on the dog's face
makes me happy, suggesting not only her intelligence
but my own, for having such a intelligent dog
in the first place. Although what it is
she wonders about I do not know. Seated in my chair,

a book in my lap, I looked up and there she was,
regarding me, as though she wondered
what this book from the library, so redolent
of others like myself, might offer me
that she herself could not. But now she seems

less inquisitive than wry, as though the compendium
of sense I find my way through, she, via the scents
only she is capable of apprehending, knows. Perhaps
someone shed a tear on a page I am yet to reach,
someone freshly washed, although the robe

she wore was not and gave traces of someone else,
someone she, the weeping woman, also sensed
in its folds, which the dog reads just as I read
the words, at this point in the volume,
not the sort anyone would cry over.

Do you want out? I ask her, and walk to the door
and open it. But she only looks up at me,
less inquisitive or wry than perplexed now,
and I begin to understand we will never understand
each other. Even when I sit on the floor

and call her to me, she seems uncertain
but allows me to stroke her head and neck
and soothe her, as she also soothes me,
although soon I rise and go back to the book,
each of us, in our own ways, unhappy.

Lucy Doolin, first day on the job, stroked his goatee
and informed the seven of us in his charge
his name was short for Lucifer, and that his father, a man
he never knew, had been possessed,
as his mother had told him, of both an odd sense of humor
and a deep and immitigable bitterness. Also
that the same man had named Lucy's twin brother,
born dead, Jesus Christ. These facts, he said,
along with his tattoos and Mohawked black hair,
we should, in our toils on his behalf, remember.

As we should also always remember to call him
only by that otherwise most womanly diminutive,
and never, he warned, by his given nor surname,
least of all with the title "mister" attached,
which would remind him of that same most hated father
and plunge him therefore into a mood
he could not promise he would, he said, "behave
appropriately within." Fortunately, our job,
unlike the social difficulties attached thereto,
was simple: collect the trash from the county's back roads.

Although, given Lucy's insistence on thoroughness,
this meant not only beer cans and bottles,
all manner of cast-off paper and plastics, but also
the occasional condom too, as well as the festering
roadkill, fresh and ridden with maggotry,
or desiccate and liftable only from the hot summer tar
with a square-bladed shovel, all of which was to be tossed

into the bed of the township truck we ourselves
rode to and from the job in. By fifty-yard increments
then we traveled. He was never not smoking a cigarette.

Late every afternoon, at the dump, while we unloaded
our tonnage of trash, he sat with Stump McCarriston,
sexton of the dump and the dump's constant resident,
in the shade, next to a green, decrepit trailer
we marveled at and strangely envied, since every inch
of wall we could see through the open door
was plastered with foldouts and pages
from every *Playboy* and nudie magazine
he had ever found among the wreckage there.
Stump, we understood, was the ugliest man on earth.

Even had Lucy not told us so, we would have known,
by the olfactory rudeness within twenty yards
of his hovel, that he never bathed. And once,
while we shoveled and scraped, he took up the .22
from beside his door and popped
with amazing accuracy three rats not fifty feet from us,
then walked to their carcasses, skinned them out,
and hung their hides on a scavenged grocery store rack
to dry. He was making, Lucy explained, a rat hide
coat we could see, come the fall, except for school.

As for school, it was a concept Stump could not fathom
and Lucy had no use for. On the truck's dash
all that summer Robert Burton's *Anatomy of Melancholy,*

a tome he said he'd read already eleven times,
this summer being the twelfth. We thought, in some way,
it might have had to do with something like the gallery
Stump's trailer contained, the first word of its title
meaning something to us, the last nothing at all.
There were things about men we might be
unable ever to know, which we somehow knew was lucky.

And Lucky, incidentally, was the name of the cat,
fat and mangy, that, once Stump was back in the shade
with Lucy, began, one by one, to consume the hideless rats.
The town we came from was sinking into the emptiness
of a thousand abandoned coal mine shafts beneath it,
and rats were more common than hares
and universally despised. They shamed us, it seemed,
as we were shamed by ignorance and curiosity—
the bodies of those women on the walls, the provenance
of rats the very earth offered up like a plague,

the burden of a name like Lucifer or Stump,
whose name, as it was scrawled on his mailbox,
seemed to be Stumplin Reilly McCarriston, Esquire.
Of the seven of us, one would die in Vietnam;
one, after medical school, would hang himself
from a beam in his parents' basement; the others
merely gone, vanished in actuality if not in memory.
Leaving me, alone, to tell this story. How Stump
would spend his last twenty years in prison,
having shot Lucy—one slender, flattening .22 slug

through the forehead—as he stood fifty feet away,
balanced atop the tub of an ancient wringer washer,
arms extended, like Jesus Christ, said Stump,
whose trailer was bulldozed into the dump itself
even before the trial, and who, no doubt, by some
court-appointed lawyer if not the appalled sheriff himself,
was forced to bathe and shave, to step into the unknown country
of a scentless white shirt and black businessman's trousers,
in order to offer his only yet most sincere defense:
that Lucifer—Mr. Doolin, as the court insisted—had told him to.

TO AUTUMN

Most beautiful aspen tree, I admire the way
a wound some buck grinding his horns

against your trunk has healed to a pale gray
that accentuates your beauty now, a decade later on.

And as today's autumn storm undresses you leaf
by delicate gold leaf, I watch until you stand

utterly bare, as we say of your kind so unsheathed.
If I'd thought, as the storm began,

that you would be less lovely uncovered,
forgive me. What did I know, just a man

watching from a window, who, having observed
and studied a wet leaf plastered against the pane,

missed, among the hundred others whirling past
in the swirl and toss of the rain, the very last.

The first four epigraphs are taken from Robert Burton, *The Anatomy of Melancholy*, New York: NYRB Classics, 2001. The fifth is from the poem "Smiles," by Wislawa Szymborska, from *View with a Grain of Sand*, New York: Harcourt, 1993.

"Friendly Fire": A V-Disc was a morale-boosting initiative involving the production of several series of recordings during World War II, by special arrangement between the United States government and various private U.S. record companies. The records were produced for use by U.S. military personnel overseas. Glenn Miller's "Moonlight Serenade" was among the most popular songs of the era. No trace has ever been found of the small plane that Miller vanished in.

"First Person": The poem referred to is "Pied Beauty." Gerard Manley Hopkins, *Selected Poems*, New York: Macmillan, 1957.

"Earthquake Light": Tohoku earthquake, Japan, March 11, 2011.

"Nightingale Capability": The poem makes use of several verbatim passages from Keats's odes, not all of which are in quotes.

"The History of Gods": See Richard Preston's article about the great trees and about research scientist Professor Stephen C. Sillet, in *The New Yorker*, February 14, 2005.

"American Archangel": "Moose," Anne Sexton, *The Complete Poems*, Boston: Houghton Mifflin, 1981.

"Socialists": KO is named for Kate Richards O'Hare, American Socialist Party activist, who was imprisoned during World War I. Eugene V. Debs: "I have no country to fight for; my country is the earth; I am a citizen of the world."

"Ain't No Use": Sarah Vaughn, *The Divine One*, CFP Domestic, 2007.

"Iris Nevis": "Eros Turannos," Edwin Arlington Robinson, *Selected Poems*, New York: Penguin, 1997.

"Anna Karenina": The opening sentence of Tolstoy's novel is, "Happy families are all alike; each unhappy family is unhappy in its own way."

ACKNOWLEDGMENTS

Brilliant Corners: Ain't No Use

Cerise Press: Legend

Chattahoochee Review: Rush

Cortland Review: The History of Gods

Fogged Clarity: Anna Karenina; Blackjack (under the title "Blackjack Imaginings"); Calendar; Catechism; The Scholar; To Autumn (under the title "Bare Tree")

The Georgia Review: Babel; Delicious

Glassworks: Dada Doodads

Little Star: Now Here

Memorious: Stop and Listen

Minnesota Review: Salvage

The New Yorker: Seen from the Porch, a Bear by the House

Poetry: Anatomy of Melancholy; Soundings

Prairie Schooner: Ode to My Boots

Shenandoah: First Person; Nightingale Capability

The Southampton Review: "American Archangel"; Socialists; The Art of Excavation

Tygerburning Literary Journal: For I Will Consider My Cat Lenore; Goldfinches; Spring Is Here

The Yale Review: On a Series of Four Photographs
"Earthquake Light" appeared in the *Global Poetry Anthol-ogy*, Montreal: Véhicule Press, 2012.

Robert Wrigley's previous books include *Beautiful Country* (2010); *Earthly Meditations: New and Selected Poems* (2006); and *Lives of the Animals* (2003). A recipient of the San Francisco Poetry Center Book Award, the Kingsley Tufts Award, and the Poets' Prize, he teaches at the University of Idaho and lives on Moscow Mountain, with his wife, the writer Kim Barnes.

Penguin Poets

JOHN ASHBERY
Selected Poems
Self-Portrait in a Convex
  Mirror

TED BERRIGAN
The Sonnets

LAUREN BERRY
The Lifting Dress

JOE BONOMO
Installations

PHILIP BOOTH
Selves

JULIANNE BUCHSBAUM
The Apothecary's Heir

JIM CARROLL
Fear of Dreaming:
  The Selected Poems
Living at the Movies
Void of Course

ALISON HAWTHORNE DEMING
Genius Loci
Rope

CARL DENNIS
Callings
New and Selected
  Poems 1974–2004
Practical Gods
Ranking the Wishes
Unknown Friends

DIANE DI PRIMA
Loba

STUART DISCHELL
Backwards Days
Dig Safe

STEPHEN DOBYNS
Velocities: New and Selected
  Poems, 1966–1992

EDWARD DORN
Way More West: New and
  Selected Poems

ROGER FANNING
The Middle Ages

ADAM FOULDS
The Broken Word

CARRIE FOUNTAIN
Burn Lake

AMY GERSTLER
Crown of Weeds: Poems
Dearest Creature
Ghost Girl
Medicine
Nerve Storm

EUGENE GLORIA
Drivers at the Short-Time Motel
Hoodlum Birds
My Favorite Warlord

DEBORA GREGER
By Herself
Desert Fathers, Uranium
  Daughters
God
Men, Women, and Ghosts
Western Art

TERRANCE HAYES
Hip Logic
Lighthead
Wind in a Box

ROBERT HUNTER
Sentinel and Other Poems

MARY KARR
Viper Rum

WILLIAM KECKLER
Sanskrit of the Body

JACK KEROUAC
Book of Sketches
Book of Blues
Book of Haikus

JOANNA KLINK
Circadian
Raptus

JOANNE KYGER
As Ever: Selected Poems

ANN LAUTERBACH
Hum
If in Time: Selected Poems,
  1975–2000
On a Stair
Or to Begin Again

CORINNE LEE
PYX

PHILLIS LEVIN
May Day
Mercury

WILLIAM LOGAN
Macbeth in Venice
Madame X
Strange Flesh
The Whispering Gallery

ADRIAN MATEJKA
Mixology

MICHAEL MCCLURE
Huge Dreams: San Francisco
  and Beat Poems

DAVID MELTZER
David's Copy: The Selected
  Poems of David Meltzer

ROBERT MORGAN
Terroir

CAROL MUSKE-DUKES
An Octave above Thunder
Red Trousseau
Twin Cities

ALICE NOTLEY
Culture of One
The Descent of Alette
Disobedience
In the Pines
Mysteries of Small Houses

LAWRENCE RAAB
The History of Forgetting
Visible Signs: New and Selected
  Poems

BARBARA RAS
The Last Skin
One Hidden Stuff

MICHAEL ROBBINS
Alien vs. Predator

PATTIANN ROGERS
Generations
Wayfare

WILLIAM STOBB
Absentia
Nervous Systems

TRYFON TOLIDES
An Almost Pure Empty Walking

ANNE WALDMAN
Gossamurmur
Kill or Cure
Manatee/Humanity
Structure of the World
  Compared to a Bubble

JAMES WELCH
Riding the Earthboy 40

PHILIP WHALEN
Overtime: Selected Poems

ROBERT WRIGLEY
Anatomy of Melancholy and Other
  Poems
Beautiful Country
Earthly Meditations: New and
  Selected Poems
Lives of the Animals
Reign of Snakes

MARK YAKICH
The Importance of Peeling
  Potatoes in Ukraine
Unrelated Individuals Forming a
  Group Waiting to Cross

JOHN YAU
Borrowed Love Poems
Paradiso Diaspora